NEAR THE OCEAN

ROBERT LOWELL
NEAR THE OCEAN

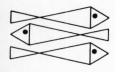

FARRAR, STRAUS AND GIROUX · NEW YORK

FOR
BLAIR CLARK

The theme that connects my translations is Rome, the greatness and horror of her Empire. My Juvenal and Dante versions are as faithful as I am able or dare or can bear to be. The Horace is freer, the Spanish sonnets freer still. How one jumps from Rome to the America of my own poems is something of a mystery to me. I want to thank my wife, Stanley Kunitz, Philip Booth, Harris Thomas, and William Arrowsmith for objections and suggestions.

R. L.

Contents

NEAR THE OCEAN

Near
the ocean

1. WAKING EARLY
SUNDAY MORNING

O to break loose, like the chinook
salmon jumping and falling back,
nosing up to the impossible
stone and bone-crushing waterfall—
raw-jawed, weak-fleshed there, stopped by ten
steps of the roaring ladder, and then
to clear the top on the last try,
alive enough to spawn and die.

Stop, back off. The salmon breaks

water, and now my body wakes

to feel the unpolluted joy

and criminal leisure of a boy—

no rainbow smashing a dry fly

in the white run is free as I,

here squatting like a dragon on

time's hoard before the day's begun!

Vermin run for their unstopped holes;

in some dark nook a fieldmouse rolls

a marble, hours on end, then stops;

the termite in the woodwork sleeps—

listen, the creatures of the night

obsessive, casual, sure of foot,

go on grinding, while the sun's

daily remorseful blackout dawns.

Fierce, fireless mind, running downhill.
Look up and see the harbor fill:
business as usual in eclipse
goes down to the sea in ships—
wake of refuse, dacron rope,
bound for Bermuda or Good Hope,
all bright before the morning watch
the wine-dark hulls of yawl and ketch.

I watch a glass of water wet
with a fine fuzz of icy sweat,
silvery colors touched with sky,
serene in their neutrality—
yet if I shift, or change my mood,
I see some object made of wood,
background behind it of brown grain,
to darken it, but not to stain.

O that the spirit could remain
tinged but untarnished by its strain!
Better dressed and stacking birch,
or lost with the Faithful at Church—
anywhere, but somewhere else!
And now the new electric bells,
clearly chiming, "Faith of our fathers,"
and now the congregation gathers.

O Bible chopped and crucified
in hymns we hear but do not read,
none of the milder subtleties
of grace or art will sweeten these
stiff quatrains shovelled out four-square—
they sing of peace, and preach despair;
yet they gave darkness some control,
and left a loophole for the soul.

No, put old clothes on, and explore
the corners of the woodshed for
its dregs and dreck: tools with no handle,
ten candle-ends not worth a candle,
old lumber banished from the Temple,
damned by Paul's precept and example,
cast from the kingdom, banned in Israel,
the wordless sign, the tinkling cymbal.

When will we see Him face to face?
Each day, He shines through darker glass.
In this small town where everything
is known, I see His vanishing
emblems, His white spire and flag-
pole sticking out above the fog,
like old white china doorknobs, sad,
slight, useless things to calm the mad.

Hammering military splendor,
top-heavy Goliath in full armor—
little redemption in the mass
liquidations of their brass,
elephant and phalanx moving
with the times and still improving,
when that kingdom hit the crash:
a million foreskins stacked like trash . . .

Sing softer! But what if a new
diminuendo brings no true
tenderness, only restlessness,
excess, the hunger for success,
sanity of self-deception
fixed and kicked by reckless caution,
while we listen to the bells—
anywhere, but somewhere else!

O to break loose. All life's grandeur
is something with a girl in summer . . .
elated as the President
girdled by his establishment
this Sunday morning, free to chaff
his own thoughts with his bear-cuffed staff,
swimming nude, unbuttoned, sick
of his ghost-written rhetoric!

No weekends for the gods now. Wars
flicker, earth licks its open sores,
fresh breakage, fresh promotions, chance
assassinations, no advance.
Only man thinning out his kind
sounds through the Sabbath noon, the blind
swipe of the pruner and his knife
busy about the tree of life . . .

Pity the planet, all joy gone
from this sweet volcanic cone;
peace to our children when they fall
in small war on the heels of small
war—until the end of time
to police the earth, a ghost
orbiting forever lost
in our monotonous sublime.

2. FOURTH OF JULY IN MAINE

(For Harriet Winslow)

Another summer! Our Independence
Day Parade, all innocence
of children's costumes, helps resist
the communist and socialist.
Five nations: Dutch, French, Englishmen,
Indians, and we, who held Castine,
rise from their graves in combat gear—
world-losers elsewhere, conquerors here!

Civil Rights clergy face again
the scions of the good old strain,
the poor who always must remain
poor and Republicans in Maine,
upholders of the American Dream,
who will not sink and cannot swim—
Emersonian self-reliance,
lethargy of Russian peasants!

High noon. Each child has won his blue,
red, yellow ribbon, and our statue,
a dandyish Union Soldier, sees
his fields reclaimed by views and spruce—
he seems a convert to old age,
small, callous, elbowed off the stage,
while the canned martial music fades
from scene and green—no more parades!

Blue twinges of mortality
remind us the theocracy
drove in its stakes here to command
the infinite, and gave this land
a ministry that would have made
short work of Christ, the Son of God,
and then exchanged His crucifix,
hardly our sign, for politics.

This white Colonial frame house,
willed downward, Dear, from you to us,
still matters—the Americas'
best artifact produced en masse.
The founders' faith was in decay,
and yet their building seems to say:
"Every time I take a breath,
my God you are the air I breathe."

New England, everywhere I look,
old letters crumble from the Book,
China trade rubble, one more line
unravelling from the dark design
spun by God and Cotton Mather—
our *bel età dell' oro*, another
bright thing thinner than a cobweb,
caught in Calvinism's ebb.

Dear Cousin, life is much the same,
though only fossils know your name
here since you left this solitude,
gone, as the Christians say, for good.
Your house, still outwardly in form
lasts, though no emissary come
to watch the garden running down,
or photograph the propped-up barn.

If memory is genius, you
had Homer's, enough gossip to
repeople Trollope's Barchester,
nurses, Negro, diplomat, down-easter,
cousins kept up with, nipped, corrected,
kindly, majorfully directed,
though family furniture, decor,
and rooms redone meant almost more.

How often when the telephone
brought you to us from Washington,
we had to look around the room
to find the objects you would name—
lying there, ten years paralyzed,
half blind, no voice unrecognized,
not trusting in the afterlife,
teasing us for a carving knife.

High New England summer, warm
and fortified against the storm
by nightly nips you once adored,
though never going overboard,
Harriet, when you used to play
your chosen Nadia Boulanger
Monteverdi, Purcell, and Bach's
precursors on the Magnavox.

Blue-ribboned, blue-jeaned, named for you,
our daughter cartwheels on the blue—
may your proportion strengthen her
to live through the millennial year
Two Thousand, and like you possess
friends, independence, and a house,
herself God's plenty, mistress of
your tireless sedentary love.

Her two angora guinea pigs
are nibbling seed, the news, and twigs—
untroubled, petrified, atremble,
a mother and her daughter, so humble,
giving, idle and sensitive,
few animals will let them live,
and only a vegetarian God
could look on them and call them good.

Man's poorest cousins, harmonies
of lust and appetite and ease,
little pacific things, who graze
the grass about their box, they praise
whatever stupor gave them breath
to multiply before their death—
Evolution's snails, by birth,
outrunning man who runs the earth.

And now the frosted summer night-dew
brightens, the north wind rushes through
your ailing cedars, finds the gaps;
thumbtacks rattle from the white maps,
food's lost sight of, dinner waits,
in the cold oven, icy plates—
repeating and repeating, one
Joan Baez on the gramophone.

And here in your converted barn,
we burn our hands a moment, borne
by energies that never tire
of piling fuel on the fire;
monologue that will not hear,
logic turning its deaf ear,
wild spirits and old sores in league
with inexhaustible fatigue.

Far off that time of gentleness,
when man, still licensed to increase,
unfallen and unmated, heard
only the uncreated Word—
when God the Logos still had wit
to hide his bloody hands, and sit
in silence, while his peace was sung.
Then the universe was young.

We watch the logs fall. Fire once gone,

we're done for: we escape the sun,

rising and setting, a red coal,

until it cinders like the soul.

Great ash and sun of freedom, give

us this day the warmth to live,

and face the household fire. We turn

our backs, and feel the whiskey burn.

3. THE OPPOSITE HOUSE

All day the opposite house,
an abandoned police stable,
just an opposite house,
is square enough—six floors,
six windows to a floor,
pigeons ganging through
broken windows and cooing
like gangs of children tooting
empty bottles.

Tonight, though, I see it shine
in the Azores of my open window.
Its manly, old-fashioned lines
are gorgeously rectilinear.
It's like some firework to be fired
at the end of the garden party,
some Spanish *casa*, luminous
with heraldry and murder,
marooned in New York.

A stringy policeman is crooked

in the doorway, one hand on his revolver.

He counts his bullets like beads.

Two on horseback sidle

the crowd to the curb. A red light

whirls on the roof of an armed car,

plodding slower than a turtle.

Deterrent terror!

Viva la muerte!

4. CENTRAL PARK

Scaling small rocks, exhaling smog,
gasping at game-scents like a dog,
now light as pollen, now as white
and winded as a grounded kite—
I watched the lovers occupy
every inch of earth and sky:
one figure of geometry,
multiplied to infinity,
straps down, and sunning openly . . .
each precious, public, pubic tangle
an equilateral triangle,
lost in the park, half covered by
the shade of some low stone or tree.
The stain of fear and poverty
spread through each trapped anatomy,
and darkened every mote of dust.
All wished to leave this drying crust,
borne on the delicate wings of lust
like bees, and cast their fertile drop
into the overwhelming cup.

Drugged and humbled by the smell
of zoo-straw mixed with animal,
the lion prowled his slummy cell,
serving his life-term in jail—
glaring, grinding, on his heel,
with tingling step and testicle . . .

Behind a dripping rock, I found
a one-day kitten on the ground—
deprived, weak, ignorant and blind,
squeaking, tubular, left behind—
dying with its deserter's rich
Welfare lying out of reach:
milk cartons, kidney heaped to spoil,
two plates sheathed with silver foil.

Shadows had stained the afternoon;
high in an elm, a snagged balloon
wooed the attraction of the moon.
Scurrying from the mouth of night,
a single, fluttery, paper kite
grazed Cleopatra's Needle, and sailed
where the light of the sun had failed.
Then night, the night—the jungle hour,
the rich in his slit-windowed tower . . .
Old Pharaohs starving in your foxholes,
with painted banquets on the walls,
fists knotted in your captives' hair,
tyrants with little food to spare—
all your embalming left you mortal,
glazed, black, and hideously eternal,
all your plunder and gold leaf
only served to draw the thief . . .

We beg delinquents for our life.
Behind each bush, perhaps a knife;
each landscaped crag, each flowering shrub,
hides a policeman with a club.

5. NEAR THE OCEAN

(For E. H. L.)

The house is filled. The last heartthrob
thrills through her flesh. The hero stands,
stunned by the applauding hands,
and lifts her head to please the mob . . .
No, young and starry-eyed, the brother
and sister wait before their mother,
old iron-bruises, powder, "Child,
these breasts . . ." He knows. And if she's killed

his treadmill heart will never rest—
his wet mouth pressed to some slack breast,
or shifting over on his back . . .
The severed radiance filters back,
athirst for nightlife—gorgon head,
fished up from the Aegean dead,
with all its stranded snakes uncoiled,
here beheaded and despoiled.

We hear the ocean. Older seas
and deserts give asylum, peace
to each abortion and mistake.
Lost in the Near Eastern dreck,
the tyrant and tyrannicide
lie like the bridegroom and the bride;
the battering ram, abandoned, prone,
beside the apeman's phallic stone.

Betrayals! Was it the first night?
They stood against a black and white
inland New England backdrop. No dogs
there, horse or hunter, only frogs
chirring from the dark trees and swamps.
Elms watching like extinguished lamps.
Knee-high hedges of black sheep
encircling them at every step.

Some subway-green coldwater flat,
its walls tatooed with neon light,
then high delirious squalor, food
burned down with vodka . . . menstrual blood
caking the covers, when they woke
to the dry, childless Sunday walk,
saw cars on Brooklyn Bridge descend
through steel and coal dust to land's end.

Was it years later when they met,
and summer's coarse last-quarter drought
had dried the hardveined elms to bark—
lying like people out of work,
dead sober, cured, recovered, on
the downslope of some gritty green,
all access barred with broken glass;
and dehydration browned the grass?

Is it this shore? Their eyes worn white
as moons from hitting bottom? Night,
the sandfleas scissoring their feet,
the sandbed cooling to concrete,
one borrowed blanket, lights of cars
shining down at them like stars? . . .
Sand built the lost Atlantis . . . sand,
Atlantic ocean, condoms, sand.

Sleep, sleep. The ocean, grinding stones,
can only speak the present tense;
nothing will age, nothing will last,
or take corruption from the past.
A hand, your hand then! I'm afraid
to touch the crisp hair on your head—
Monster loved for what you are,
till time, that buries us, lay bare.

For
Theodore Roethke

1908–1963

All night you wallowed through my sleep,
then in the morning you were lost
in the Maine sky—close, cold and gray,
smoke and smoke-colored cloud.

Sheeplike, unsociable reptilian, two
hell-divers splattered squawking on the water,
loons devolving to a monochrome.
You honored nature,

helpless, elemental creature.

The black stump of your hand

just touched the waters under the earth,

and left them quickened with your name. . . .

Now, you honor the mother.

Omnipresent,

she made you nonexistent,

the ocean's anchor, our high tide.

1958

Remember standing with me in the dark,
escaping? In the wild house? Everything—
I mad, you mad for me? And brought my ring
that twelvecarat lunk of gold there . . . Joan of Arc,
undeviating still to the true mark?
Robust, ah taciturn! Remember playing
Marian Anderson, Mozart's *Shepherd King,*
il re pastore? Hammerheaded shark,
the rainbow salmon of the world—your hand
a rose . . . And at the Mittersill, you topped
the ski-run, that white eggshell, your sphere, not land
or water—no circumference anywhere,
the center everywhere, I everywhere,
infinite, fearful . . . standing—you escaped.

Spring

(Horace, *Odes*, Book I, 4: *Solvitur acri hiems*)

Sharp winter melts and changes into spring—
now the west wind, now cables haul the boats
on their dry hulls, and now the cattle tire
of their close stalls, the farmer of his fire.
Venus leads dancers under the large moon,
the naked nymphs and graces walk the earth,
one foot and then another. Birds return,
they flash and mingle in mid-air. Now, now,
the time to tear the blossoms from the bough,
to gather wild flowers from the thawing field;
now, now, to sacrifice the kid or lamb
to Faunus in the green and bursting woods,
for bloodless death with careless foot strikes down
the peasant's hut and the stone towers of kings.

Move quickly, the brief sum of life forbids

our opening any long account with hope;

night hems us in, and ghosts, and death's close clay . . .

Sestius, soon, soon, you will not rush to beat

the dice and win the lordship of the feast,

or tremble for the night's fatiguing joys,

sleepless for this child, then for that one—boys

soon lost to man, soon lost to girls in heat.

Serving under Brutus

(Horace, *Odes*, Book II, 7: *O saepe mecum tempus in ultimum*)

O how often with me in the forlorn hope
under the proconsulship of Marcus Brutus,
Citizen! Who brought you back to Rome,
to our sultry gods and hot Italian sky?

My first friend, and my best, O Pompey,
how often have we drawn out the delaying day
with wine, and brightened our rough hair,
with Syrian nard!

With you too at Philippi, at that hysterical
mangling of our legions, when we broke
like women. Like an Egyptian,
I threw away my little shield.

I was afraid, but Mercury, the quick,

the subtle, found a way for me to escape.

And you? The wave of battle drew you under,

knocked you down into its troubled, bleeding surf.

Offer the Sky-god then this meal,

spread out your flesh worn out by war.

Enjoy this laurel tree, and don't forget me,

or spare the wine jars set aside for you.

Fill the frail goblets with red wine,

pour perfume from the fragile shells!

Who'll be the first to twist parsley

and myrtle with the coronets?

Throw down the dice. Throw down the dice—

Venus has chosen her master of the feast.

I'll drink like Alexander. It is sweet

to drink to fury when a friend's reprieved.

Cleopatra

(Horace, *Odes*, Book I, 37: *Nunc pede liberum*)

Now's the time to drink,

to beat the earth in rhythm,

toss flowers on the couches of the gods,

Friends!

Before this, it was infamous

to taste the fruit of the vine,

while Cleopatra with her depraved gangs,

germs of the Empire, plotted

to enthrone her ruin in the Capitol,

and put an end to Rome . . .

Impotent,

yet drunk on fortune's favors . . .

but Caesar tamed your soul:

you saw with a now sober eye

the scowling truth of his terror,

O Cleopatra, scarcely escaping,

and with a single ship, and scarcely

escaping from your limping fleet, on fire,

Cleopatra, with Caesar running on the wind,

three rising stands of oars, with Caesar

falling on you like a sparrow hawk

fallen on some soft dove or sprinting rabbit

in the winter field. And yet you sought

a more magnanimous way to die.

Not womanish, you scorned our swords,
you did not search for secret harbors.
Regal, resigned and anguished,
Queen, you even saw your house in ruin.

Poisonous snakes gave up their secrets,
you held them with practiced hands,
you showed your breasts. Then bolder, more ferocious,
death slipping through your fingers,

how could you go aboard Octavian's galleys,
how could you march on foot, unhumbled,
to crown triumphant Caesar's triumph—
no queen now, but a private woman?

The vanity
of human wishes

A VERSION OF JUVENAL'S TENTH SATIRE

(For William Arrowsmith)

In every land as far as man can go,

from Spain to the Aurora or the poles,

few know, and even fewer choose what's true.

What do we fear with reason, or desire?

Is a step made without regret? The gods

ruin whole households for a foolish prayer.

Devoured by peace, we seek devouring war,

the orator is drowned by his torrential speech,

the gladiator's murdered by his skill

at murder. Wealth is worse; how many pile

fortune on fortune—like the Atlantic whale,

they bulk above the lesser fish and die.

For this in the dark years and at the word

of Nero, Seneca's high gardens fell;
Longinus died; a cohort of praetorians
besieged the Laterani. No soldiers purge
a garret. If you take a walk at night,
carrying a little silver, be prepared
to think each shadow hides a knife or spear.
You'll fear each wavering of the moonlit reed,
while beggars whistle in the robber's face.

Almost the first and last prayer made in all
the temples is for wealth: "Let my estate
stand first in Rome!" But who drinks arsenic
from earthenware? Fear death each time you lift
the jewelled goblet, or when vintage wine
purples the golden bowl.

Which wise man shall
I praise, Democritus or Heraclitus,
he who smiled or he who wept each time
he left his house? But the dry smilé comes easy,
I marvel any finds sufficient tears.
Democritus could laugh till he was sick,
and yet in those days in his little town,
there were no fasces, litters, canopies,
no tribune bawling from the tribunal.
What if he'd seen the praetor riding high
in his triumphal car across the Circus,
dragging his palm-embroidered robes of Zeus,
a gold-stitched toga, and a cloud of dust?
What if he'd seen him in his cardboard crown,
a millstone that no mortal neck could bear—
there elbowed by a sweating German slave,
crowding the praetor to deflate his pride?
And now the eagle on its ivory staff,
the hornblowers, the herd of toadies mixed

with citizens of Rome, in snow-white robes,

his dearest friends, the lackeys in his pay.

Democritus could laugh at everything;

his neighbors' self-importance made him smile,

he even found amusement in their tears,

and by his courage and good humor proved

that honesty and wisdom can survive

the smothering air of a provincial town.

When Superstition shouted for his head,

he laughed, and left her hanging in her noose.

Why do we hunger so for vicious things?

Our wishes bend the statues of the gods.

How many men are killed by Power, by Power

and Power's companion, Envy! Your long list

of honors breaks your neck. Statues follow

the rope and crash, the axe cuts down the two-
wheeled chariot's wheels and snaps the horse's legs.
Fierce hiss the fires, the bellows roar, the head,
all-popular and adored by all once, burns—
Sejanus crackles, and his crude bronze face,
the second in the world, melts down to jars,
frying pans, basins, platters, chamber pots.
Hang out your streamers, lead the great chalked bull
to the high altar at the Capitol—
men lead Sejanus on a hook, and all
rejoice. "What flannel lips he has! No man,
I tell you, ever loved this man!" "But tell us,
what was his crime, friend? Who were the informers?
What witness swore away his life?" "No witness!
A wordy long epistle came from Capri."
"Tiberius spoke, enough, I'll hear no more."
But what about the Roman mob? Their rule

is always follow fortune and despise
the fallen. One thing's certain, if the gods
had spared Sejanus, if some accident
had choked Tiberius in his green old age,
the mob would hail Sejanus Caesar now.

Now that we have no suffrage left to sell,
we have no troubles; we who once conferred
legions, fasces, empires, everything,
are simply subjects; restlessly we ask
for two things: bread and circuses. But listen—
"I hear that many more are going to die."
"No doubt about it, they have built a fire."
"My closest friend, Brutidius, looked white
just now at Mars's altar, Caesar stirs,
I fear fresh heads will fall for negligence."
"Quick, Caesar's enemy is still exposed;

let's run; there's time to trample on the corpse."
"I'll bring my slaves for witnesses; no paid
accuser shall drag me haltered into court."
Thus, thus, the secret murmurs of the crowd—
would you be cheered and flattered like Sejanus?
Be rich as Croesus, give the ivory chair
to one, and armies to another? Would you be
Tiberius' right hand, while he sits and suns
himself at Capri, fed by eastern fags?
Surely you'd like to have his lances, cohorts,
blue-blooded knights and army corps of slaves.
Why not, friend? Even if you never wished
to murder, you would like to have the power.
But would you want to glitter and rise this high,
if ruin's counterweight must crush your life?

Who would prefer Sejanus' rod of office
to being mayor of Gabii, or Fidenae,
some rural aedile smashing crooked weights,
wearing a threadbare cloak at Ulubrae?
Let's say then that Sejanus was insane;
wanting authority and wealth, he added
story on story to his towering house—
so much the higher for the blinding crash!
What ruined Crassus, Pompey, he who scourged
Gaul and the torn Republic with his lash?
What brought them down? High places and the art
of climbing, wishes answered by the gods,
who send few kings to Pluto without wounds,
still fewer cherished by their people's love.

                        Each schoolboy

who cultivates Minerva with a penny fee,

and one poor slave to lug his satchel, prays through

the summer holidays for eloquence,

to be Demosthenes or Cicero.

Yet eloquence destroyed both orators,

this, this condemned and drowned them in its flood.

Eloquence lopped off Cicero's right hand,

and cut his throat, but no cheap shyster ever

dirtied the Roman rostrum with his blood.

"My consulate, how fortunate the state":

if this were all you wrote, you might have scorned

the swords and vengeance of Antonius.

Yes, all in all, I like such pompous verse

more than your force, immortal fifth Philippic!

Dark too the murder of the patriot Greek,

who stunned the men of Athens with his words,

and held the hushed assembly in his palm.

Under unfriendly gods and an ill star,

your blacksmith father raised and sent you forth,

red-eyed and sooty from the glowering forge,

from anvil, pincers, hammer and the coals

to study rhetoric, Demosthenes!

War souvenirs and trophies nailed to trees,

a cheek strap dangling from a clobbered helmet,

a breastplate, or a trireme's figurehead,

or captives weeping on the victor's arch:

these are considered more than human prizes.

For these Greek, Roman, and barbarian

commanders march; for these they pledge their lives

and freedom—such their thirst for fame, and such

their scorn of virtue, for who wants a life

of virtue without praise? Whole nations die

to serve the glory of the few; all lust

for honors and inscriptions on their tombs—

those tombs a twisting fig tree can uproot,
for tombs too have their downfall and their doom.

Throw Hannibal on the scales, how many pounds
does the great captain come to? This is he
who found the plains of Africa too small,
rich Carthage with her mercenary grip
stretched from Gibraltar to the steaming Nile
and back to Ethiopia, her stud
for slaves and elephants. He set his hand
firmly on Spain, then scaled the Pyrenees;
when snows, the Alps, and Nature blocked his road,
he derricked rocks, and split the mountainsides
with vinegar. Now Italy is his;
the march goes on. "Think nothing done," he says,
"until my Punic soldiers hack through Rome,
and plant my standard over the Suburva's
whorehouses." What a face for painters! Look,

the one-eyed leader prods his elephant!
And what's the end? O glory! Like the others,
he is defeated, then the worried flight,
the great, world-famous client cools his heels
in royal anterooms, and waits on some
small despot, sleeping off a drunken meal.
What is the last day of this mighty spirit
whose valor turned the known world on its head?
Not swords, or pikes, or legions—no, not these,
his crown for Cannae and those seas of blood
is poison in a ring. March, madman, cross
the Alps, the Tiber—be a purple patch
for schoolboys, and a theme for declamation!

One world was much too small for Alexander,
racing to gain the limits of the globe,
as if he were a circling charioteer;

early however he reached his final city,

Babylon, fortified with frail dry brick.

A grave was all he wanted. Death alone

shows us what tedious things our bodies are.

Fleets climbed the slopes of Athos (such the lies

of Greek historians) yes, and paved the sea;

wheels rumbled down a boulevard of decks,

breakfasting Persians drank whole rivers dry—

that's how the perjured laureates puffed their songs.

But tell us how the King of Kings returned

from Salamis? Xerxes, whose amusement was

whipping the winds, and bragging how he'd drag

Neptune in chains, and branded to his throne—

a lovely master for the gods to serve!

Tell us of his return. A single ship,

scything for sea-room through the Persian dead.

That was his sentence for his dreams of glory.

"Give us long life, O God, and years to live,"
in sickness or in health, this is our prayer;
but age's ills are strong and never fail.
Look at the face, deformed and paralyzed,
unlike itself, its skin a hide, gone cheeks,
a thousand wrinkles like a mother ape.
But youth's unique: each boy is handsomer
than the next one, or cleverer, or stronger;
all old men look alike, their voices shake
worse than their fingers, every head is hairless,
each snivels like a child; they mess their bread,
their gums are toothless—how heavily they weigh
upon their wives, their children, and themselves!
Even the fortune-hunter turns them down,
now food and even wine are one more torture,
a long oblivion falls on intercourse,
the shy nerve, pumping, drops like a wet leaf,
though tickled through the night, it cannot rise.

What do you hope from your white pubic hairs?
Sex hounds you, when its power is gone. Or take
the loss of other senses—the best voice
strikes on the coughing ear like lead, the harp
of the best harpist screams like a ground knife.
What good are bosoms jingling with gold coins,
the best seat in the Colosseum, when you
can hardly tell a trumpet from a drum?
The boy announcing visitors or meals
half kills himself with baying in your ear.

Now only fevers warm the thinning blood,
diseases of all kinds lock hands and dance,
even their names escape you—let me list
the many lechers Oppia will love,
slow-coming Maura drain a day, how many
schoolboys Hamillus will crouch on, the partners
Hirrus will swindle, the sick men Themiston will kill

this autumn—I could more easily count

the villas bought up by the barber whose

razor once grated on my stiff young beard . . .

One man has a sagging shoulder, one a hernia,

another has a softening hipbone, and another

has cataracts; another's spoonfed: listen,

they yawn like baby swallows for their swill!

But the worst evil is the loss of mind;

we do not know our slaves, the friend we dined with,

then even our own children are forgotten.

"Who are they? Parasites!" The will's rewritten:

All goes to Phiale, so lulling are

the acrobatics of that quick, moist mouth

that used to sell her body in the streets.

Let's say you keep your mind, you'll live to see

your wife and sons laid out, the ashes of

brothers and sisters shut in marble urns.

These the rewards of living long: repeated
groaning that fills an empty house, yourself
in black, a ghost, disaster on disaster!
Nestor, if one believes the lines from Homer,
lived longer than a crow—how fortunate,
outwitting death and tasting the new wine
a hundred autumns! Was this all? Fate's grace,
and his long thread of years were all too much
for Nestor. He saw the beard of his son, Antilochus,
flame on the pyre, asked: "Why have I lived? What crime
have I committed?" Peleus felt the same
for his Achilles, and Laertes for
Odysseus. What of Priam? Would that he had died
the day when Paris launched his robber galley;
he would have met his city's shades, with Troy
still standing, Hector and all his sons on hand
to bear him on their shoulders, with Cassandra,
unravished, free to wail the song of mourning.

What good was his long life? He saw his house
fallen, all Asia burning—swords, then fire!
Then dropping his tiara, and putting on
armor, the poor old doddering soldier rushed
before the altar of his gods, and fell
like some old ox discarded by the plow,
craning his thin neck for the master's knife.
But Priam's death was human; Hecuba
survived him to die barking like a dog.

I pass by Mithridates; why repeat
Solon's old saws to Croesus—take our own men,
take Marius. Age brought him prison, exile,
weeks on his belly in Minturnae's marsh,
then back to Rome, his seventh consulship,
a few brief apoplectic days of blood.
Did Nature ever raise a Roman higher?
Did Rome? if he had died with all the pomp

of war, his army marshalled out to cheer him,
one foot descending on a Teuton's back?
How provident was the Campanian fever
for Pompey; but the tears of many cities,
all praying for his life, prevailed. He lived,
his stars preserved him, and a eunuch's slave
cut off his head. Was Lentulus so tortured?
Was Cethegus? Or even Catiline,
whose corpse lay undishonored on the field?

The nervous mother passing Venus' altar
prays for good-looking sons and lovelier daughters.
"Why not?" she says. "Latona bore Diana!"
Why not? And yet Lucretia's fate forbids
us to desire her face. Virginia
would swap her figure for Rutila's hump.
A handsome son has shy and trembling parents.
Luck seldom goes with beauty. But suppose

a simple household teaches him the fathers'
virtues and Sabine manners, say that nature
moreover makes him kind, intelligent,
with warm blood rising to his cheeks—
what better gifts can nature give the boy,
all-giving nature, gentler than his teachers?
And yet the boy will never be a man.
Some prodigal seducer will seduce
the parents—money never fails its giver.
No overweight tyrant castrates the deformed.
Trust Nero, Nero had an eye for beauty:
he never picked a spastic or a lout.

Let's say your son survives, and reaches twenty.
He'll look for softer and more practiced hands
than Nero's. He will fly to women. Would
you have him an adulterer like Mars,
almost as handsome, but no luckier,

his bronze foot kicking in the cripple's net?
Risk the worst punishments the laws allow
an injured husband? Often the revenge
outdoes the law: the cuckold chops the lover's
balls off, or jams a mullet up his arse.
Then let him choose a widow; soon he'll have
her money, all her unloved body has
to give. What can Catulla, what can Chloris
deny his swelling prick—sad sacks in heat,
their conscience washing out between their legs.
But beauty never hurts the good! Go ask
Bellerophon, go ask Hippolytus.
Chastity couldn't save their lives from Phaedra,
or Sthenoboea, faithful wives, then scorned
lovers screwed on to murder by their shame.

Now tell me what advice you have to give
the fellow Caesar's consort wants to marry—
the best man, the most beautiful, an old
patrician house could raise, soon caught, soon shoved
from life to death by Messalina's eyes.
She's long been seated, and her bridal veil
rustles, the lovers' bed of full-blown roses
rustles quite openly inside the garden;
by ancient rule, a dowry of a million
brass sesterces must now be counted—clerks,
lawyers, the thin-lipped priest, attend on tiptoe.
"What, did you want a hole-in-corner marriage?
The lady has a right to her religion.
What will you do? Speak up! Say no, you'll die
before the lamps are lit. Say yes, you'll live
until the city hears, and someone squeals
in Claudius's ear—he'll be the last in Rome
to know of his disgrace. Meanwhile obey

your love, if one or two days' life mean much—
whatever's best or costs the smallest effort,
to bring your fair white body to the sword."

There's nothing then to pray for? If you pray,
pray for the gods and Jupiter to help.
What's best, what serves us, only He can know.
We're dearer to the gods than to ourselves.
Hurried by impulse and diseased desire,
we ask for wives, and children by our wives—
what wives, what children, heaven only knows.
Still, if you ask for something, if you must
buy holy sausages and dedicate
the tripe of bulls at every altar, pray for
a healthy body and a healthy soul,
a soul that is not terrified by death,
that thinks long life the least of nature's gifts,
courage that takes whatever comes—this hero

like Hercules, all pain and labor, loathes

the lecherous gut of Sardanapalus.

Success is worshipped as a god; it's we

who set up shrines and temples in her name.

I give you simply what you have already.

Brunetto Latini

CANTO XV OF DANTE'S "INFERNO"
(*For Lillian Hellman*)

And now we walked along the solid mire
above a brook whose fuming mist protected
water and banks from the surrounding fire.
Just as the men of Flanders threw up huge
earthworks to stop the sea that always threatens
their fields and cattle between Ghent and Bruges,
or Paduans along the Brenta spread
out dykes to shield their towns and towers against
spring thawing the Carinzian watershed—
on such a plan the evil engineer,
whoever he was, had laid his maze of dykes,
though on a smaller scale, and with less care.
By now we'd gone much deeper underground,
and left the bleeding wood so far behind
I'd have seen nothing, if I'd looked around.

We met a company of spirits here,

trooping below us on the sand. Each one

stared closely at our faces. As men peer

at one another under the new moon,

or an old tailor squints into his needle,

these puckered up their brows and glowered. Soon,

I saw a man whose eyes devoured me, saying,

"This is a miracle." He seized my sleeve,

and as I felt his touch, I fixed my eyes

with such intensity on his crusted face

that its disfigurement could not prevent

my recognizing who he was. "Oh, Oh,"

I answered groaning, as I stretched my hand

to touch his arm, "are you here Ser Brunetto?"

He answered, "Do not be displeased, my Son,

if Brunetto Latini turn and walk a little

downward with you, and lets this herd pass on."

Then I, "I'll go with you, or we can sit

here talking as we used to in the past,

if you desire it, and my guide permit."

"O Son," he answered, "anyone who stands
still a moment will lie here a hundred years,
helpless to brush the sparks off with his hands.
Move on, I'll follow. Soon enough I must
rejoin my little group of friends who walk
with me lamenting their eternal lust."
Then since I dared not leave my bank and move
over the flames of his low path, I bent
my head to walk with reverence and love.
Then he, "What brings you here before your day?
Is it by accident, or Providence?
Who is this man who guides you on your way?"
I answered, "In the world that lies serene
and shining over us, I lost my path,
even before the first young leaves turned green.
Yesterday morning when my steps had come
full circle, this man appeared. He turned me round,
and now he guides me on my journey home."
"O Son," said he, "if you pursue your star,
you cannot fail to reach the glorious harbor.

And if the beautiful world, less sinister,

had let me live a little longer, I too

might have sustained your work and brought you comfort,

seeing how heaven has befriended you.

But that perverted and ungrateful flock

that held the hills with Catiline, and then

descended, hard and sterile as their rock,

to govern Florence, hate you for the good

you do; and rightly! Could they wish to see

the sweet fig ripen on their rotten wood?

Surely, they've earned their reputation: blind,

fratricidal, avaricious, proud.

O root their filthy habits from your mind!

Fortune will load such honors on your back

that Guelph and Ghibelline will hunger for you.

But beat them from the pasture. Let the pack

run loose, and sicken on the carcasses

that heap the streets, but spare the tender flower,

if one should rise above the swamp and mess—

some flower in which the fragile, sacred seed

of ancient Roman virtue still survives

in Florence, that vulture's nest of lies and greed."

"Master," I said, "you would not walk here now

cut off from human nature, if my prayers

had had an answer. I remember how

I loved you, sitting at your knees—all thought

fixed on your fatherly and gentle face,

when in the world, from hour to hour, you taught

me how a man becomes eternal. O

Master, as long as I draw breath and live,

men shall remember you and what I owe.

Your words about my future shall remain

with other prophecies I keep to give

a Lady, who if I reach her, will explain.

This much I know: If I can bear the stings

of my own heavy conscience, I will face

whatever good or evil Fortune brings.

This promise of good fortune has been made

before this; so, let Fortune whirl her wheel

at random, and the peasant work his spade."

Then Virgil, turning backward with one hand

lifted in wonder, mused at me, and said:

"He who knows how to listen shall understand."

Dwelling upon his words, I did not stop

eagerly briefing Ser Brunetto, and asked,

"Who are the most illustrious in your group?"

And he, "It's right to know a few of us,

but fitting I be silent on the rest;

our time's too short to squander on such dross.

In one word, we were scholars in our time,

great men of letters, famous in the world

we soiled and lost for our one common crime.

Priscian goes with us on this dismal turf,

and Francesco d'Accorso; you can see,

if you have any liking for such scurf,

the man the Servants' Servant chose to serve

him on the Arno, then on the Bacchilione,

where he laid down his ill-extended nerve.

I would say more to you, but must not stand
forever talking, speech must have an end.
I see fresh steam is stirring from the sand,
and men I would avoid are coming. Give
me no pity. Read my *Tesoro*. In
my book, my treasure, I am still alive."

Then he turned back, and he seemed one of those
who run for the green cloth through the green field
at Verona . . . and seemed more like the one
who wins the roll of cloth than those who lose.

The Ruins of Time

(Quevedo, *Miré los muros de la patria mía* and

       Buscas en Roma a Roma, ¡O peregrino!)

(Góngora, *Esta que admiras fábrica, esta prima* and

       Menos solicitó veloz saeta)

I

I saw the musty shingles of my house,

raw wood and fixed once, now a wash of moss

eroded by the ruin of the age

turning all fair and green things into waste.

I climbed the pasture. I saw the dim sun drink

the ice just thawing from the bouldered fallow,

woods crowd the foothills, seize last summer's field,

and higher up, the sickly cattle bellow.

I went into my house. I saw how dust

and ravel had devoured its furnishing;

even my cane was withered and more bent,

even my sword was coffined up in rust—

there was no hilt left for the hand to try.

Everything ached, and told me I must die.

II

You search in Rome for Rome? O Traveller!
in Rome itself, there is no room for Rome,
the Aventine is its own mound and tomb,
only a corpse receives the worshipper.
And where the Capitol once crowned the forum,
are medals ruined by the hands of time;
they show how more was lost to chance and time
than Hannibal or Caesar could consume.
The Tiber flows still, but its waste laments
a city that has fallen in its grave—
each wave's a woman beating at her breast.
O Rome! From all your palms, dominion, bronze
and beauty, what was firm has fled. What once
was fugitive maintains its permanence.

III

This chapel that you gaze at, these stern tombs,

the pride of sculpture . . . Stop here, Passer-by,

diamonds were blunted on this porphyry,

the teeth of files wore smooth as ice. This vault

seals up the earth of those who never felt

the earth's oppression. Whose? If you would know,

stand back and study this inscription. Words

give marble meaning and a voice to bronze.

Piety made this chapel beautiful,

and generous devotion binds these urns

to the heroic dust of Sandoval,

who left his coat of arms, once five blue stars

on a gold field, to climb with surer step

through the blue sky, and scale the golden stars.

IV

The whistling arrow flies less eagerly,
and bites the bull's-eye less ferociously;
the Roman chariot grinds less hurriedly
the arena's docile sand, and rounds the goal . . .
How silently, how privately, we run
through life to die! You doubt this? Animal
despoiled of reason, each ascending sun
dives like a cooling meteorite to its fall.
Do Rome and Carthage know what we deny?
Death only throws fixed dice, and yet we raise
the ante, and stake our lives on every toss.
The hours will hardly pardon us their loss,
those brilliant hours that wore away our days,
our days that ate into eternity.